Twenty to Make

Polymer Clay Buttons

Karen Walker

Search Press

First published in Great Britain 2013

Search Press Limited
Wellwood, North Farm Road,
Tunbridge Wells, Kent TN2 3DR

Text copyright © Karen Walker 2013

Photographs by Mark Winwood at
Search Press Studios

Photographs and design copyright
© Search Press Ltd 2013

Print ISBN: 978-1-84448-880-3
EPUB ISBN: 978-1-78126-169-9
Mobi ISBN: 978-1-78126-170-5
PDF ISBN: 978-1-78126-171-2

Suppliers
If you have difficulty in obtaining any of the
materials and equipment mentioned in this
book, then please visit the Search Press website
for details of suppliers: www.searchpress.com

Printed in Malaysia

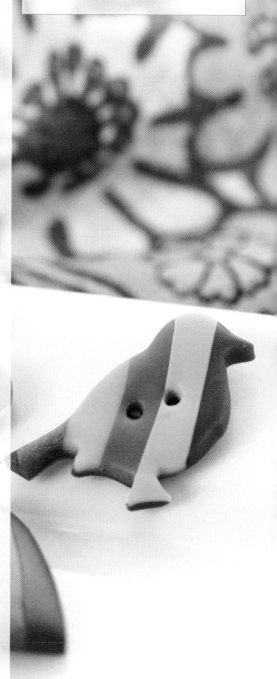

Dedication
*I dedicate this book to my beautiful
children, Jacob and Lyla.*

Contents

Introduction

All of the buttons in this book are made using polymer clay. Polymer clay is modelling clay which is permanently hardened when baked in a normal domestic oven. With stunning colours to choose from, polymer clay is perfect for both novice and expert alike. It is also extremely versatile – it can be put on to glass, wood and metals, and can be used for creating your own unique buttons!

Buttons are a great way to customise your clothes but they can also be used as embellishments on handmade cards or scrapbooks. Try threading some raffia or string through the holes before gluing them to your cards. Buttons can also be used to create unique pieces of jewellery.

You can make the buttons in this book with some simple but very effective techniques, and they are all explained in clear steps. Also included are some tips on how to make variations of the projects in order to help you to make your own buttons exactly as you want them. Experiment to familiarise yourself with each individual technique, and you will soon gain confidence through experience and begin to elaborate accordingly.

The colours of some of the buttons in this book are simply the polymer clay itself, but I have also used acrylic paints on some of the projects. For the button holes I have used cocktail sticks pushed through using a pushing and turning method; this must be done very slowly so as not to distort your button.

I think polymer clay is the perfect material for creating your own unique buttons, and with the current trend to customise your clothes, bags and scarves, it really is the ideal choice.

Tools and techniques

The tools and techniques in this book have been kept to a minimum to ease the process for both novice and experienced modeller alike. Some of the tools listed can be substituted for everyday household implements; such as a glass tumbler instead of a roller, jar lids instead of cutters, cotton reels instead of embossing tools, and baking trays instead of ceramic tiles.

Essential tools and materials:

Polymer clay You will need a selection of standard 56g (2oz) blocks.

Work surface An ideal work surface should be something that is non-porous, such as a glass chopping board or place mat, or you could use a large ceramic tile. Whatever you choose, always ensure that the surface is clean and free from dust: baby wipes are the best thing to use for cleaning.

Baby wipes Baby wipes are a must when handling your clay as they are good for keeping your work surface clean and also great for cleaning your hands in between using different colours. They can also be used for cleaning your other tools such as blades, rollers, pasta machine and cutters.

Kitchen paper It is a good idea to keep kitchen paper handy for drying your hands, work surface and all tools.

Basic tools:

Pasta machine or **roller** This is used to flatten the clay. You could also use a wine bottle or glass tumbler. If you are using a pasta machine then the thickest setting on the machine is the perfect thickness for your buttons.

Polymer clay blade This is used to cut the clay.

Sugarcraft cutters I have chosen cutters in sizes ranging from small to standard button sizes, and in a variety of shapes – hearts, circles, flowers, birds and more: the choice is yours. All cutters can be obtained from craft shops or sugarcraft suppliers.

Ceramic tile This can be used both as a work surface and to bake your finished items upon.

Acrylic block These are usually used for rubber stamping, but are used here for flattening and shaping your buttons.

Cocktail sticks These small wooden or plastic sticks are ideal for making holes, patterns and indentations in your buttons.

Additional materials:

Acrylic paints and **paintbrushes** These are used to add coloured detail.

Varnish If you are using acrylic paint on the buttons then you will need to use varnish so that it does not come off when the items go through the washing machine. Nail polish is a good alternative.

Jump rings These are small metal rings used to press into the back of the buttons. They are usually used for jewellery making.

Cotton buds Small plastic rods with cotton wool on either end, these are used for applying colour with acrylic paints.

Embossing tools These are used to emboss the clay with interesting patterns. Common household items such as cotton reels are useful.

Preparing polymer clay

Before handling the clay ensure that your hands are clean and the surface that you are working on is clean and free from dust.

Begin by softening the clay with your hands. I like to use a pasta machine as well as my hands, but this is not compulsory. This softening of the clay is referred to as conditioning. All polymer clays need to be conditioned when first taken out of their protective packets to ensure their pliability, which is paramount in ensuring success. Some colours, being harder than the others, need a little extra time. If the clay is a little hard then it can take around five to ten minutes to achieve the required consistency.

If the clay has not been conditioned properly you will not achieve good results. Above all, take your time, experiment and have fun with this versatile polymer clay!

Blending colours

Polymer clay comes in a wide variety of colours which can be blended to create other colours. I have used lots of pastel colours in this book which can be created by mixing your desired colour with an equal amount of white. The product can be purchased at most good craft shops and is widely available online.

Thickness

The thickness of your buttons is important; polymer clay is strong when baked, but can be weak if too thin. If you are using a poly roller or tumbler, then your buttons need to be at least 3mm (⅛in) thick.

Baking times

Polymer clay needs to be baked once you are finished, and instructions are included with the packaging. Baking temperatures differ throughout the range of polymer clays, therefore your baking times will differ, especially when the size of the items varies. For small items like the buttons in this book, my suggestion would be to bake them for half the recommended time as there is a tendency for the item to change colour if overdone.

Washing the buttons

Polymer clay buttons can be washed in your washing machine as long as the temperature is no higher than thirty degrees. It is important to note that polymer clay is totally unsuitable for tumble drying.

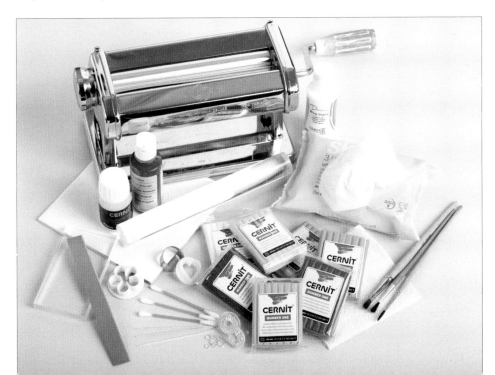

Groovy Owl

Materials:

Burgundy or dark red polymer clay blocks
Small amount of pink polymer clay
Tiny amounts of white and brown polymer clay
Brown and white acrylic paint
Varnish for the eyes and wings

Tools:

Pasta machine or roller
Polymer clay blade
30mm (1⅛in) circle cutter for the button
20mm (¾in) heart shaped or circle cutter
Cocktail sticks
Small soft paintbrush
Ceramic tile or baking tray

Instructions:

1 Begin by softening the burgundy clay you need for your button, then roll it out using a pasta machine or roller. Your rolled out piece should be at least 3mm (⅛in) thick.

2 Using a 30mm (1⅛in) diameter circle cutter, cut out your shape.

3 To create the ears, pinch the top of the circle with your fingers while pulling upwards slightly.

4 For the eyes, take a small amount of white clay and roll it into two small ball shapes. Press down on each with your finger to flatten them. Make a criss cross design on the white circles using your blade (see detail).

5 Place these circles on to the owl, and in the centre of each, place a small amount of brown clay, flattened in the same way as the white parts of the eyes.

6 For the wings, roll out a small amount of pink clay. This should be around 1mm (1/16in) thick.

7 Using a smaller 20mm (¾in) diameter circle cutter or heart shape, cut out a shape from the pink clay and cut it in half with the blade. Place these two halves on to the owl as wings.

8 Use your blade to cut out a small triangle shape from the pink clay to create the beak. Place the beak on to the owl.

9 Before baking your owl, gently press down on all the pieces that you have attached to ensure they are firmly in place.

10 Make three holes in the centre of the button using a cocktail stick, slowly turning it as you push so you do not distort the shape. Place the button on to a ceramic tile and bake following the instructions on the clay packet.

11 Once your button is cool, use a cocktail stick dipped into dark brown acrylic paint to create the polka dots on the wings, and white acrylic paint for the highlight on the eyes.

12 When the acrylic paint has dried (this can take around thirty minutes) apply one coat of varnish to the wings and eyes using a small, soft paintbrush.

For a different look, try swapping the colours to a cool turquoise or cheerful yellow.

Leopard Print

Materials:

Terracotta polymer clay block

Small amount of dark brown and black polymer clay

Tools:

Pasta machine or roller

35mm (1⅜in) circle cutter

Cocktail sticks

Ceramic tile or baking tray

Instructions:

1 Roll out the terracotta clay using the widest setting on your pasta machine. If using a roller, then make sure the clay is at least 3mm (⅛in) thickness.

2 Roll out small amounts of dark brown and black clay very thinly.

3 Pick up the black clay and begin to tear away small amounts, these pieces should all be different in size and should all have uneven edges (see detail).

4 Repeat the same process with the dark brown.

5 Start to arrange the black pieces on to the terracotta clay, making sure that you leave spaces in between. Next, place the dark brown pieces over the top of the black pieces making sure that you can still see lots of black around the edges.

6 Use your roller to gently roll over the whole piece to even out any bumps.

7 Use the 35mm (1⅜in) diameter circle cutter to cut out your leopard print button.

8 Use a cocktail stick to make your button holes, slowly turning the stick as you push. I have made four holes for these 35mm (1⅜in) diameter buttons. However, if your buttons are smaller then two holes are enough.

9 Place the button on to a ceramic tile or baking tray. Following the instructions on the packet, bake until hard.

Experiment using different colours to create different animal prints. For example, try brown and white spots for a giraffe print or orange and black stripes for a tiger print.

Pretty Flower

Materials:

Yellow polymer clay block
Small amount of brown polymer clay
Brown acrylic paint
Varnish

Tools:

Pasta machine or roller
Flower shaped cutter
Cocktail stick
Soft paintbrush
Ceramic tile or baking tray

Instructions:

1 Roll out yellow clay using the thickest setting on your pasta machine. If using a roller, then your clay needs to be around 3mm (⅛in) thick.

2 Using a flower-shaped cutter, cut out your button.

3 For the flower centre, take a small amount of brown clay and roll it in your palms to make a ball shape. Flatten it by pressing down gently with one finger, then place it into the centre of your flower button.

4 Use a cocktail stick to make two holes in the centre of the flower about 1mm (¹⁄₁₆in) apart. Turn the stick as you slowly push it through to avoid distorting the shape of the flower.

5 Place the flower button on to a ceramic tile or baking tray and bake it until it is hard, following the instructions on the packet.

6 Once your flower button has cooled, decorate it with polka dots using a cocktail stick dipped into a small amount of brown acrylic paint (see detail).

7 When the paint is completely dry, add one coat of varnish using a soft paintbrush.

These buttons would look great on a child's cardigan or sewn on to a hat, scarf or gloves. Try embossing the surface with patterns, as in the pink example at the top of the picture.

Sweetheart

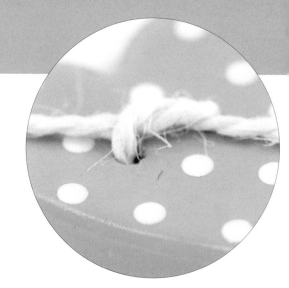

Materials:

Pink and white polymer clay blocks

White acrylic paint

Varnish

String

Tools:

Pasta machine or roller

Heart shaped cutter

Cocktail stick

Ceramic tile or baking tray

Soft paintbrush

Instructions:

1 Mix equal amounts of white polymer clay with pink polymer clay to produce a pastel hue.

2 Roll out the pastel clay using a pasta machine or roller to around 3mm (⅛in) thickness.

3 Using a heart shaped cutter to cut out your button.

4 For the button holes make two holes, roughly 1mm (¹⁄₁₆in) apart with a cocktail stick. Turn the stick as you slowly push it through so that you do not distort the button.

5 Place the button on to a ceramic tile or baking tray and bake until it is hard.

6 Once your button has completely cooled take a cocktail stick and dip the tip into a small amount of acrylic paint. Touch it to the button to create a polka dot design on your heart, reloading the tip when you run out of paint.

7 Once the acrylic paint has dried completely, apply one coat of varnish using a soft paintbrush and allow to dry.

8 To finish, thread string through the buttonholes and tie a loose knot (see detail).

These cute hearts can be used individually, or strung together. Try using different coloured string to set off your own sweetheart buttons.

Woven Button

Materials:

White, turquoise and brown polymer clay blocks

Tools:

30mm (1⅛in) diameter circle cutter
Cocktail stick
Ceramic tile or baking tray
Polymer clay blade

Instructions:

1 Begin by softening your three different coloured polymer clays as described on page 7.

2 Once your clay is soft, begin to roll each piece slowly into a 3mm (⅛in) thick strand. Each of the three strands should be around 220mm (8¾in) in length.

3 Lay the three strands side by side and squeeze them together at one end only.

4 First take the strand on your right and take it over the middle strand, then take your left strand over your right strand (this method is the same as plaiting or braiding hair). Keep the braid quite tight so there are no gaps in between the strands.

5 Repeat this method until you reach the end of the braid.

6 Gently press your braid together then cut it into three equal parts with the polymer clay blade.

7 Lay the three parts side by side and gently press them together to make a solid piece.

8 Take your circle cutter and cut out a button from the piece.

9 Using a cocktail stick, make two holes in the centre of your button around 2mm (³⁄₃₂in) apart. Turn the stick as you slowly push it through to avoid distorting the button.

10 Place the button on to a ceramic tile or baking tray and bake until it is hard, following the instructions on the packet.

Try using just two strands instead of three; or twist the two strands together, instead of braiding, for a completely different look.

Psychedelic

Materials:

Scrap pieces (pieces left over from other
    projects) of polymer clay in several colours

Tools:

Polymer clay blade

Acrylic block or ceramic tile

Cocktail stick

Heart shaped cutter

Ceramic tile or baking tray

Instructions:

1 Take a small handful of polymer clay scraps and begin to
squeeze them together in your hand. Do not roll the clay as this
will mix the colours together.

2 Once the pieces have joined together, start to squeeze them
into a small fat sausage shape.

3 Hold the sausage shape in two hands and twist the whole
piece several times.

4 Place the twisted sausage on to your work surface and
gently flatten it a little using an acrylic block or the
shiny side of a ceramic tile.

5 Press down hard on the whole piece with your
acrylic block to flatten it to a thickness of 3mm
(⅛in). Do not roll out the piece as this will distort
the unique pattern.

6 Using a heart cutter, cut out a shape and make
two holes in the centre using a cocktail stick,
turning it as you push slowly, in order to not distort
the pattern.

7 Place the button on a ceramic tile or baking tray
and follow the instructions on the packet to bake until
hard, then allow it to cool to finish.

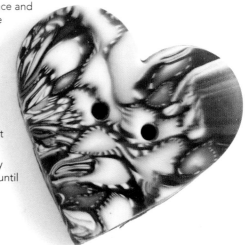

Every button you make this way will be one of a kind! For a button that has lots of pattern you will need a variety of colours and lots of tiny pieces rather than big pieces.

To make a symmetrical button, take your blade and make a single cut down the centre of your block of clay after step 4. Take the two halves and open them like a book to reveal a mirror image. Place these two halves side by side and gently press them together before continuing with steps 5–7.

Ladybird

Materials:
Red and black polymer clay blocks
Varnish
Jump ring

Tools:
Polymer clay blade
Cocktail stick
Ceramic tile or baking tray
Soft paintbrush

Instructions:

1 Roll a 14mm (½in) diameter ball of red polymer clay, then flatten it slightly with your finger to form a dome shape. This will be the body of the ladybird.

2 Use your blade to cut off a small piece at the front, leaving a flat edge.

3 Make a smaller ball with the black polymer clay and flatten it with your fingers.

4 Cut the black piece in half and attach one of theses pieces to the flat part of the body.

5 With a cocktail stick or blade, make a line across the centre of the red part. This will mark out the wing cases.

6 For the spots, roll pieces of black polymer clay into tiny balls and place them on to the red body, pressing down with your finger to flatten them.

7 Place a tiny amount of black in between the wings just underneath so that a small amount shows through.

8 Use a cocktail stick to make two eyes.

9 Press a jump ring gently into the underside of your ladybird. To make sure the jump ring stays in your button; press a tiny amount of clay through the jump ring and press down firmly (see detail) to secure it in place.

10 Place your ladybird on to a ceramic tile and bake until hard, following the instructions on the packet.

11 Once cooled, varnish the button with a soft paintbrush and leave to dry.

The jewel-like sheen and colours of ladybirds means that they look beautiful as the basis for button designs. A group of these buttons makes a pretty addition to this picture frame.

Toadstool

Materials:

Red and white polymer clay blocks

Varnish

Jump ring

Tools:

Ceramic tile or baking tray

Soft paintbrush

Instructions:

1 Roll out a 6mm (¼in) diameter ball of red clay, then flatten it with your finger.

2 Begin to form a toadstool shape and put to one side.

3 Take a smaller amount of white clay and roll into a ball, flatten slightly and form into a stalk shape.

4 Attach the two shapes together.

5 Make tiny balls of white clay and place them on to the red part of the toadstool, pressing them in to flatten and secure them to the red part.

6 Press a jump ring into the back of the toadstool and secure it with a tiny amount of clay pushed through the ring (see detail).

7 Place the button on a baking tray and bake in the oven until hard, then cool.

8 Once your button has cooled, varnish it using a soft brush and leave to dry.

Strung together on ribbon, these perky buttons have hundreds of uses around the home, but they would also look gorgeous on gloves or a scarf.

Chunky Square

Materials:

White, light blue, blue and
   dark blue polymer clay blocks

Tools:

Polymer clay blade

Pasta machine or roller

Cocktail stick

Ceramic tile or baking tray

Instructions:

1 Use a roller or pasta machine to roll out all four colours separately. Each piece needs to be around 1mm (1/16in) thick.

2 Place each colour on top of each other in this order: light blue, blue, white, dark blue (see detail).

3 Using your blade, cut out a 25 x 25mm (1 x 1in) square.

4 Use a cocktail stick to make the button holes, twisting and pushing so that you do not distort the shape of the square.

5 Place your button on to a ceramic tile or baking tray and bake until hard, following the instructions on the packet. Allow to cool.

24

Any shape that has straight sides will give a great geometrical effect! If you are making more than one of these buttons I suggest making a template using a piece of card to ensure that they are the same size.

Russian Doll

Materials:

Blue, red and white polymer clay blocks

Small amounts of dark brown and flesh-coloured polymer clay

Varnish

White, red, pink and black acrylic paint

Tools:

Pasta machine or roller

Cocktail stick

Soft paintbrush

Small paintbrush

Cotton bud

Ceramic tile or baking tray

Instructions:

1 Roll some blue clay into a 14mm (½in) diameter ball.

2 Press down on the ball with your finger to create a pear shape.

3 Roll a small amount of flesh-coloured clay into a ball then flatten it with your finger. Place this on to the head part of the doll.

4 Roll out 10mm (⅜in) diameter balls of white and red clay into 30mm (1⅛in) strands.

5 Lay the white strand on to the doll just underneath the chin (but not touching the chin itself). Flatten the white strand a little.

6 Use a cocktail stick to make small lines going across the white strand. Repeat this process with the red strand, making different patterns using a cocktail stick. Trim off any bits that hang over the sides using your blade.

7 For the scarf, roll out two tiny amounts of blue clay and press them in between your fingers. Squeeze at one end to form a leaflike shape. Use a cocktail stick to create the crease in the scarf. Place these two pieces underneath the chin.

8 For the hair, roll two small amounts of dark brown clay into balls. Flatten them with a finger, then create leaf shapes by squeezing each at one end. Place these on to the doll's head.

9 Make two holes in the centre of your doll with a cocktail stick, just underneath the scarf. Turn the stick as you make the hole.

10 Place the buttons on a ceramic tile or baking tray. Following the instructions on the packet, bake the buttons to set them hard, then allow them to cool.

11 Once cooled, use a cocktail stick dipped into white acrylic paint to create polka dots on the scarf around the hair and dress.

12 Dip a cocktail stick into black acrylic paint and add two eyes (see detail).

13 Paint on a red mouth using a very small paintbrush. Use a cotton bud with a very small amount of pink paint for the cheeks.

14 Once the acrylic paint has dried, use the soft paintbrush to apply one coat of varnish to all of the painted parts and to the hair.

Experiment using different colours patterns and textures! Use these buttons to make jewellery such as necklaces and bracelets.

Spots

Materials:

Dark brown polymer clay block

Small amounts of red, turquoise, orange, yellow and purple polymer clay

Tools:

Pasta machine or roller

Flower shaped cutter

Cocktail stick

Ceramic tile or baking tray

Instructions:

1 Roll out some dark brown clay to around 3mm (⅛in) thickness using a pasta machine or roller.

2 Roll the red, turquoise, orange, yellow and purple polymer clay into tiny balls. You will need roughly three or four of each colour.

3 Place the tiny balls of colour on to the brown piece of polymer clay, then press each one down using your finger.

4 Gently roll the whole piece with your roller to smooth out the surface and firmly embed the other colours without smearing them (see detail).

5 Using a flower shaped cutter, carefully cut out your button.

6 Use a cocktail stick to make two holes in the centre, roughly 1mm (⅛in) apart, for the button holes. Twist as you push the stick through so you do not distort the button.

7 Place the button on a ceramic tile or baking tray and bake until hard, following the instructions on the packet. Allow to cool.

This design lends itself well to all kinds of shapes. Instead of using a flower cutter, try using heart or circle cutters.

Vintage

Materials:

Terracotta polymer clay blocks
Small amount of turquoise polymer clay

Tools:

Cocktail stick
Acrylic block or ceramic tile
Ceramic tile or baking tray

Instructions:

1 Roll a 12mm (½in) diameter ball of terracotta clay, then flatten it to a thickness of 3mm (⅛in) using an acrylic block or the smooth side of a ceramic tile.

2 Roll a small amount of turquoise clay into a ball and flatten it with your finger, this needs to be around 1.5mm (³⁄₃₂in) thick.

3 Place the turquoise circle in the centre of the terracotta circle and gently press it into place (see detail).

4 Use a cocktail stick to create tiny grooves all the way around the terracotta part, and to make two button holes in the centre of the turquoise circle. Make the holes 1mm (¹⁄₁₆in) apart, and turn the stick as you push it through the button.

5 Place your vintage button on to a ceramic tile or baking tray and bake it until it is hard, following the instructions on the packet. Allow the button to cool.

You can use almost anything to emboss your polymer clay buttons. Vintage buttons, with their interesting decorative shapes, are especially good for this.

Pawprint

Materials:

Stone effect or grey polymer clay block

Black polymer clay block

Varnish

Black acrylic paint

Tools:

Pasta machine or roller

30mm (1⅛in) diameter circle cutter

Cocktail stick

Ceramic tile or baking tray

Fine paintbrush

Soft paintbrush

Instructions:

1 Roll out your grey stone effect clay using a pasta machine or roller to around 3mm (⅛in) thickness.

2 Using the 30mm (1⅛in) circle shaped cutter, cut out the base of your button and put it to one side.

3 Roll a small amount of black clay into a ball, then use your finger to flatten and shape it into the main part of the pawprint. Place this into the centre of your button base.

4 Roll smaller amounts of black clay into four balls, then flatten and place them on to the button as shown for the toes.

5 With a cocktail stick make two button holes, roughly 1mm (¹⁄₁₆in) apart.

6 Place the button on to a ceramic tile and bake it until hard, following the instructions on the packet.

7 Once the button has completely cooled, paint on some claws with black acrylic paint using a fine paintbrush (see detail).

8 Use the soft paintbrush to apply a coat of matt or gloss varnish over the claws to protect the paint.

Try doing different pawprints by varying the shape of the main part and altering the number of toes. You could also add a little glitter to the black polymer clay for a sparkly effect.

Piggy

Materials:

Flesh coloured and pale pink polymer clay blocks

Dark brown, red and pale pink acrylic paint

Varnish

Tools:

Acrylic block

Cocktail stick

Cotton bud

Fine paintbrush

Soft paintbrush

Ceramic tile or baking tray

Instructions:

1 Begin by softening your flesh coloured clay and rolling it into a 17mm (⅝in) ball.

2 Using your acrylic block, press down firmly on the ball of clay to flatten it to around 3mm (⅛in) thick.

3 For the snout, roll a small amount of pale pink clay into a ball and flatten it using your finger.

4 Roll out two smaller balls of pink clay then flatten them. Pinch each at one end to form the pig's ears.

5 Place the snout in the centre of the button, then place the ears, making sure the ears curve over the edge of the main shape a little (see detail).

6 Make two holes through the centre of the snout with a cocktail stick, using a pushing and turning method to ensure clean holes all the way through the button without distorting the shape.

7 Place the button on to a ceramic tile or baking tray. Following the instructions on the packet, bake the button to set it hard, then allow it to cool.

8 Once cooled, dip a cocktail stick into some dark brown acrylic paint then touch it to the button for the eyes.

9 Use a fine paintbrush to paint a small mouth with the dark brown paint. Use a cotton bud with a very small amount of pale pink for the cheeks.

10 When the paint has dried, use the soft paintbrush to apply a coat of varnish over the painted areas.

Reversing the colours, so you use pink for the main shape and flesh for the ears and nose, will give a more vibrant effect.

Rainbow

Materials:

Red, turquoise, orange, yellow
   and purple polymer clay blocks

Tools:

Pasta machine or roller

Polymer clay blade

Heart shaped cutter

Cocktail stick

Ceramic tile or baking tray

Instructions:

1 Use the pasta machine or roller to roll out some red clay to 1.5mm (³⁄₃₂in) thickness. Put this to one side.

2 Roll out some red, turquoise, orange, yellow and purple clay to 1.5mm (³⁄₃₂in) thickness.

3 Use your blade to cut 4mm (¼in) wide, 4cm (1½in) long strips of each colour.

4 Place each strip on to your rolled-out red piece, starting with a red strip then turquoise, orange, yellow and purple, making sure all the strips are directly next to each other with no gaps in between.

5 Use your finger to gently smooth the strips together into a solid surface (see detail).

6 Using a heart shaped cutter, cut out your button at an angle so that you can see all five colours.

7 Turning a cocktail stick as you push it in, make two button holes, roughly 1mm (¹⁄₁₆in) apart.

8 Place the button on to a ceramic tile and bake until hard, following the instructions on the packet.

For a different look, try cutting wider or narrower strips of colour, or using different shaped cutters.

Songbird

Materials:

Pale blue, yellow and orange polymer clay blocks
Red, blue, white and brown acrylic paint
Varnish

Tools:

Acrylic block
Cocktail stick
Cotton bud
Fine paintbrush
Soft paintbrush

Instructions:

1 Roll some pale blue clay into a 14mm (½in) diameter ball.

2 Flatten the ball using an acrylic block. Begin to shape the bird by pinching the flattened ball with your fingers at one end to form a leaf shape.

3 Bend the pointed end (the tip of the leaf) a little so that it sticks up like shown.

4 Roll a tiny amount of yellow clay into a ball and form it into a leaf shape. This will be the beak.

5 Score a line in the beak using a cocktail stick.

6 Roll a small amount of orange into a ball, then flatten and shape it in the same way to make the wing.

7 Attach all the pieces together, then make two button holes with a cocktail stick, turning it as you push it through.

8 Place on a ceramic tile or baking tray and bake until hard, following the instructions on the packet.

9 Once cooled, use a cocktail stick dipped into white acrylic paint to create polka dots on the wing. Paint the eyes with the cocktail stick using white and brown acrylic paint.

10 Dip the cotton bud into red acrylic paint and wipe away the excess. Use the remaining paint to add a blush to the cheeks and beak.

11 Using a fine paintbrush, paint tiny lines all the way around your bird button (see detail).

12 Once the acrylic paint has dried, apply one coat of varnish to the entire button using a soft brush.

Try adding different designs to the wings. You could also try making the wings textured by using embossing tools.

Nautical

Materials:

Red, white and blue polymer clay blocks

Tools:

Pasta machine or roller
30mm (1⅛in) diameter circle cutter
Cocktail stick
Ceramic tile or baking tray
Polymer clay blade

Instructions:

1 Roll out some red clay using the thickest setting on your pasta machine. If using a roller, then make sure the clay is at least 3mm (⅛in) thick.

2 Using the 30mm (1⅛in) diameter circle cutter, cut out your button. Put it to one side.

3 Roll some white and blue clay into long strands.

4 Twist the two strands together and wind them around the edge of your button. Use the polymer clay blade to cut the ends where they will meet.

5 Ensuring you have a blue part meeting a white part, press the ends together gently to join them (see detail).

6 Gently press the strands to secure them to the button, then make two holes in the centre of the red part using a cocktail stick.

7 Place the button on a ceramic tile or baking tray and bake until hard, following the instructions on the packet. Allow to cool.

For a different but complementary nautical look, try swapping the colours around.

Black and White

Materials:

Black and white polymer clay blocks

Tools:

Pasta machine or roller
Polymer clay blade
Cocktail stick
30mm (1⅛in) diameter circle cutter
Ceramic tile or baking tray

Instructions:

1 Roll out some black clay using a pasta machine or roller. Your rolled out piece should be at least 3mm (⅛in) thick. Put this to one side.

2 Use the pasta machine or roller to roll sheets of black clay and white clay as thinly as you can.

3 Place these two thin sheets on top of each other. With your blade cut out a 70 x 40mm (2¾ x 1½in) piece.

4 Roll this piece into a swiss roll (US jelly roll) until you have a 10mm (½in) diameter roll. You can make thinner rolls for smaller slices.

5 With your polymer clay blade, slice around fourteen thin slices from your swiss roll.

6 Place these slices on to the rolled out piece of black polymer clay from step 1.

7 Press down over the whole piece with your acrylic block to even out any bumps (see detail).

8 Use the 30mm (1⅛in) circle cutter to cut out your button, then make two holes using a cocktail stick, roughly 2mm (³⁄₃₂in) apart. Turn the cocktail stick as you make the holes, and push it through slowly to keep the pattern intact.

9 Place the button on a ceramic tile or baking tray. Following the instructions on the packet, bake until hard. Allow to cool.

This is a very simple idea using just two colours. Even without using more, different shapes can give different effects.

Cupcake

Materials:

Red and white polymer clay blocks

White acrylic paint

Varnish

Tools:

Pasta machine or roller

Polymer clay blade

Cocktail stick

Jump ring

Ceramic tile or baking tray

Soft and fine paintbrushes

Instructions:

1 Roll out the red clay, using a pasta machine or roller, to around 3mm (⅛in) thickness.

2 Cut out a 20mm (¾in) square from the sheet of red clay using your blade. Cut off the edges of the red square with your blade to make a cupcake case shape as shown.

3 Make the ridges on the cupcake case piece by pressing the length of a cocktail stick firmly into the clay (see detail).

4 Roll some white clay into a sausage shape and cut it into three different size pieces, one 20mm (¾in), one 12mm (½in) and one 7mm (¼in) in length. Put the icing together by laying the longest piece at the bottom and the shortest piece on the top.

5 Use a cocktail stick to create the ridges on the icing piece by pressing the side of it in (see detail).

6 For the cherry, roll a small amount of red clay into a ball.

7 Attach all the pieces together.

8 Press a jump ring into the back of your cupcake (see step 9 on page 20). To make sure the jump ring stays in your button, press a tiny amount of clay through the jump ring and press down firmly.

9 Place your cupcake on to a ceramic tile and bake until hard, following the instructions on the packet.

10 Once your button has completely cooled, take a cocktail stick and dip the tip into a small amount of white acrylic paint. Touch it to the cupcake case part to create a polka dot design. Use a fine paintbrush to paint a highlight on the cherry.

11 Once the acrylic paint has dried, use the soft paintbrush to apply one coat of varnish to the polka dotted areas and to the cherry.

Decorate your cupcake buttons by using tiny beads on the frosting. You can also use a larger bead or polymer clay flower in place of the polymer clay cherry.

Antique

Materials:

Burgundy or dark red polymer clay blocks

White acrylic paint

Gold metallic acrylic paint

Varnish

Raffia

Tools:

Pasta machine or roller

Embossing tools, such as a cotton reel or a piece of jewellery

Heart shaped cutter

Cocktail stick

Stiff bristle paintbrush

Soft paintbrush

Kitchen towel

Ceramic tile or baking tray

Instructions:

1 Roll out your burgundy clay to 3mm (⅛in) thickness using a pasta machine or roller.

2 With your embossing tool, press down firmly into the clay to make a random pattern.

3 Using a heart shaped cutter cut out your button.

4 For the button holes make two holes, roughly 1mm (¹⁄₁₆in) apart, by pushing a cocktail stick slowly through the button, while turning it.

5 Place the button on to a ceramic tile or baking tray. Following the instructions on the packet, bake until hard.

6 Once your button has completely cooled, take a stiff bristle paintbrush and dip it into a tiny amount of white acrylic paint.

7 Wipe the brush on to some kitchen paper as if you were trying to wipe the colour off the brush.

8 Brush over the button several times to achieve the desired effect. You are aiming to catch the upper surfaces of the design but to still be able to see the burgundy clay in the recesses (this technique is referred to as drybrushing).

9 Repeat the same process with some gold metallic paint.

10 Once the paint has dried, apply one coat of varnish using a soft paintbrush.

11 To finish, thread raffia through the buttonholes and tie a loose knot (see detail) once the varnish has dried completely.

There are lots of things around the home that can be used to emboss your buttons such as old pieces of jewellery, vintage buttons and items found in the kitchen drawer! Experiment using different colour clays and paints.

Acknowledgements

A huge thank you to my wonderful family and friends for all their support and love! Also a big thank you to all at Search Press for making this happen for me!

Publisher's note

For more information, you are invited to visit the author's blog:
www.karen-walker.org

If you would like more books on polymer clay modelling, try the following:
Twenty to Make: Polymer Clay Bears
by Birdie Heywood, Search Press 2010
Twenty to Make: Tasty Trinkets
by Charlotte Stowell, Search Press 2010